AUSTIN VJ MAKO

WARFARE
PRAYERS

**515 PRAYER
SCRIPTURES**

**ITS TIME TO WIN
THAT BATTLE**

DEDICATION

I have put together 515 Prayer scriptures that can be used by anyone and see the hand of God move.

This book is dedicated to both my mums Sylvia **M'hango & Cathrine Ndaiseka**

May you enjoy this easy-to-read and easy-to-pray booklet. May the same God who has answered me also answer your prayers. May He answer by fire, by the wind, by water, by His name and any other way that will fulfil God's desire in your lives.

Thank you for the love, care, and all protection you provided for me.

I love you both.

Shalom

Austin the 316

CONTENT

INTRODUCTION

Here in your hand is a very powerful weapon ready to be used against any power, Throne, principality, witch, wicked ruler etc. I have shared 515 scriptures that will bring instant and permanent Victory. I pray that the LORD will teach you how to use these arrows to shoot at your target and get results. May your prayer language change, and may you move to a higher level.

Firing Squad!

Make Ready!

AIM!

FIRE!

EXCEEDINGLY BEYOND EXPECTATIONS

Y ou will go from expectation to manifestation. This month is a month for your divine shift and laughter.

1.   Ephesians 3:20-21

20 Now to Him who is able to do exceedingly abundantly above all that we ask or think, according to the power that works in us, 21 to Him be glory in the church by Christ Jesus to all generations, forever and ever. Amen.

2. Genesis 48:18

And Joseph said to his father, "Not so, my father, for this one is the firstborn; put your right hand on his head."

3. Joel 2:26

You shall eat in plenty and be satisfied,
And praise the name of the Lord your God,
Who has dealt wondrously with you;
And My people shall never be put to shame

4. Romans 8:28

And we know that all things work together for good to those who love God, to those who are called according to His purpose.

5. Psalm 126:2

Then our mouth was filled with laughter,
And our tongue with singing.
Then they said among the nations,
"The Lord has done great things for them.

6. **1 Samuel 3:11**

   Then the Lord said to Samuel: "Behold, I will do something in Israel at which both ears of everyone who hears it will tingle.

7. **Genesis 38:29**

   Then it happened, as he drew back his hand, that his brother came out unexpectedly; and she said, "How did you break through? This breach be upon you!" Therefore, his name was called Perez.

8. **Genesis 26:22**

   And he moved from there and dug another well, and they did not quarrel over it. So he called its name Rehoboth, because he said, "For now the Lord has made room for us, and we shall be fruitful in the land."

9. **Job 22:25**

   Yes, the Almighty will be your gold and your precious silver;

10. **Deuteronomy 28:11**

    And the Lord will grant you plenty of goods, in the fruit of your body, in the increase of your livestock, and in the produce of your ground, in the land of which the Lord swore to your fathers to give you.

11. **Proverbs 10:22**

    The blessing of the Lord makes one rich,
    And He adds no sorrow with it.

12. **Genesis 26:13**

The man began to prosper, and continued prospering until he became very prosperous;

13. 2 Chronicles 25:9

Then Amaziah said to the man of God, "But what shall we do about the hundred talents which I have given to the troops of Israel?"
And the man of God answered, "The Lord is able to give you much more than this."

14. Ecclesiastes 9:11

I returned and saw under the sun that—
The race is not to the swift,
Nor the battle to the strong,
Nor bread to the wise,
Nor riches to men of understanding,
Nor favor to men of skill;
But time and chance happen to them all.

15. Psalm 102:13

You will arise and have mercy on Zion;
For the time to favor her,
Yes, the set time, has come.

FINANCIAL DELIVERANCE

We intercept, and we override evil imaginations. (heaven, church, mind). Let Every attack on my financial and *destiny helpers be aborted.*

1. **2 Corinthians 10:5**
   casting down arguments and every high thing that exalts itself against the knowledge of God, bringing every thought into captivity to the obedience of Christ,

2. *Proverbs 19:21*
   There are many plans in a man's heart,
   Nevertheless the Lord's counsel—that will stand.

3. **Hosea 9:14**
   Give them, O Lord—
   What will You give?
   Give them a miscarrying womb
   And dry breasts!

4. **Luke 1:24**
   Now after those days, his wife Elizabeth conceived; and she hid herself five months, saying,

5. **James 1:17**
   Every good gift and every perfect gift is from above, and comes down from the Father of lights, with whom there is no variation or shadow of turning.

6. **2 Samuel 9:3**
   Then the king said, "Is there not still someone of the house of Saul, to whom I may show the kindness of God?"

And Ziba said to the king, "There is still a son of Jonathan who is lame in his feet."

7. Jeremiah 49:39

'But it shall come to pass in the latter days:
I will bring back the captives of Elam,' says the Lord."

8. Psalm 50:10

For every beast of the forest is Mine,
And the cattle on a thousand hills.

9. Isaiah 45:3

I will give you the treasures of darkness
And hidden riches of secret places,
That you may know that I, the Lord,
Who call you by your name,
Am the God of Israel.

10. Jeremiah 41:8

But ten men were found among them who said to Ishmael, "Do not kill us, for we have treasures of wheat, barley, oil, and honey in the field." So he desisted and did not kill them among their brethren.

11. Ezekiel 27:24-25

24 These were your merchants in choice items—in purple clothes, in embroidered garments, in chests of multi-coloured apparel, in sturdy woven cords, which were in your marketplace.
25 "The ships of Tarshish were carriers of your merchandise. You were filled and very glorious in the midst of the seas.

PRAYER

cancel every evil decree that is delaying the manifestation of my testimony. I override, overpower every demonic road block working against my testimony.

12. Lamentations 3:37

Who is he who speaks and it comes to pass,
When the Lord has not commanded it?

13. Isaiah 14:27

For the Lord of hosts has purposed,
And who will annul it?
His hand is stretched out,
And who will turn it back?"

14. Luke 1:45

Blessed is she who believed, for there will be a fulfilment of those things which were told her from the Lord."

15. Zechariah 4:7

'Who are you, O great mountain?
Before Zerubbabel you shall become a plain!
And he shall bring forth the capstone
With shouts of "Grace, grace to it!"

16. Romans 8:35 – 39

35 Who shall separate us from the love of Christ? Shall tribulation, or distress, or persecution, or famine, or nakedness, or peril, or sword? 36 As it is written:

"For Your sake we are killed all day long;
We are accounted as sheep for the slaughter."
37 Yet in all these things we are more than conquerors through Him who loved us.
38 For I am persuaded that neither death nor life, nor angels nor principalities nor powers, nor things present nor things to come, 39 nor height nor depth, nor any other created thing, shall be able to separate us from the love of God which is in Christ Jesus our Lord.

17. Psalm 3:1-3
1 Lord, how they have increased who trouble me!
Many are they who rise up against me.
2 Many are they who say of me,
"There is no help for him in God." Selah

3 But You, O Lord, are a shield for me,
My glory and the One who lifts up my head.

18. 1 Kings 5:4
But now the Lord my God has given me rest on every side; there is neither adversary nor evil occurrence.

19. Numbers 23:23
"For there is no sorcery against Jacob,
Nor any divination against Israel.
It now must be said of Jacob
And of Israel, 'Oh, what God has done!'

20. Jeremiah 11:21-22

21 "Therefore thus says the Lord concerning the men of Anathoth who seek your life, saying, 'Do not prophesy in the name of the Lord, lest you die by our hand'—
22 therefore thus says the Lord of hosts: 'Behold, I will punish them. The young men shall die by the sword, their sons and their daughters shall die by famine;

21. Jeremiah 15:21

"I will deliver you from the hand of the wicked,
And I will redeem you from the grip of the terrible."

22. Esther 9:1

Now in the twelfth month, that is, the month of Adar, on the thirteenth day, the time came for the king's command and his decree to be executed. On the day that the enemies of the Jews had hoped to overpower them, the opposite occurred, in that the Jews themselves overpowered those who hated them.

In the end you win

23. 1 Corinthians 15:57

But thanks be to God, who gives us the victory through our Lord Jesus Christ.

24. Proverbs 21:31

The horse is prepared for the day of battle,
But deliverance is of the Lord.

25. Ecclesiastes 9:11

I returned and saw under the sun that—

The race is not to the swift,
Nor the battle to the strong,
Nor bread to the wise,
Nor riches to men of understanding,
Nor favor to men of skill;
But time and chance happen to them all.

26. Romans 8:37

Yet in all these things we are more than conquerors through Him who loved us.

27. 1 John 5:4

For whatever is born of God overcomes the world. And this is the victory that has overcome the world—our faith.

28. 2 Kings 5:1

Now Naaman, commander of the army of the king of Syria, was a great and honorable man in the eyes of his master, because by him the Lord had given victory to Syria. He was also a mighty man of valor, but a leper.

29. 1 Kings 18:46

Then the hand of the Lord came upon Elijah; and he girded[a] up his loins and ran ahead of Ahab to the entrance of Jezreel.

30. John 20:4-5

4 So they both ran together, and the other disciple outran Peter and came to the tomb first.
5 And he, stooping down and looking in, saw the linen cloths lying there; yet he did not go in.

31. Joshua 7:4 – 5

4 So about three thousand men went up there from the people, but they fled before the men of Ai.

5 And the men of Ai struck down about thirty-six men, for they chased them from before the gate as far as Shebarim, and struck them down on the descent; therefore the[d] hearts of the people melted and became like water.

32. Joshua 8:1-2

1 Now the Lord said to Joshua: "Do not be afraid, nor be dismayed; take all the people of war with you, and arise, go up to Ai. See, I have given into your hand the king of Ai, his people, his city, and his land.

2 And you shall do to Ai and its king as you did to Jericho and its king. Only its spoil and its cattle you shall take as booty for yourselves. Lay an ambush for the city behind it."

33. Jeremiah 30:16-17

16 Therefore all those who devour you shall be devoured;
And all your adversaries, every one of them, shall go into captivity;
Those who plunder you shall become plunder,
And all who prey upon you I will make a prey.
17 For I will restore health to you
And heal you of your wounds,' says the Lord,
'Because they called you an outcast saying:
"This is Zion; No one seeks he

34. Nahum 2:9

Take spoil of silver!
Take spoil of gold!
There is no end of treasure,
Or wealth of every desirable prize.

15

35. Psalm 23:5

You prepare a table before me in the presence of my enemies;
You anoint my head with oil;
My cup runs over.

36. James 1:17-18

17 Every good gift and every perfect gift is from above, and comes down from the Father of lights, with whom there is no variation or shadow of turning.
18 Of His own will He brought us forth by the word of truth, that we might be a kind of firstfruits of His creatures.

37. Genesis 24:12

Then he said, "O Lord God of my master Abraham, please give me success this day, and show kindness to my master Abraham.

THANKSGIVING PRAYERS THAT USHER TIMES OF REFRESHING

O'Lord, I thank you for the fact that I am still here against all odds.

38.   2 Samuel 22:50
Therefore I will give thanks to You, O Lord, among the Gentiles,
And sing praises to Your name.

39. 1 Chronicles 16:8
Oh, give thanks to the Lord!
Call upon His name;
Make known His deeds among the peoples!

40. 1 Chronicles 16:34
Oh, give thanks to the Lord, for He is good!
For His mercy endures forever.

41. Psalm 6:5
For in death there is no remembrance of You;
In the grave who will give You thanks?

42. Psalm 30:12
To the end that my glory may sing praise to You and not be silent.
O Lord my God, I will give thanks to You forever.

43. Psalm 106:47
Save us, O Lord our God,
And gather us from among the Gentiles,
To give thanks to Your holy name,

To triumph in Your praise.

44. Psalm 107:1
Oh, give thanks to the Lord, for He is good!
For His [a]mercy endures forever.

45. Psalm 119:62
At midnight I will rise to give thanks to You,
Because of Your righteous judgments.

46. Matthew 15:36
And He took the seven loaves and the fish and gave thanks, broke them and gave them to His disciples; and the disciples gave to the multitude.

47. Luke 17:16
and fell down on *his* face at His feet, giving Him thanks. And he was a Samaritan.

48. 2 Corinthians 2:14
Now thanks be to God who always leads us in triumph in Christ, and through us diffuses the fragrance of His knowledge in every place.

49. 1 Corinthians 15:57
But thanks be to God, who gives us the victory through our Lord Jesus Christ.

50. 2 Corinthians 9:15
Thanks *be* to God for His indescribable gift!

51. Colossians 1:12

giving thanks to the Father who has qualified us to be partakers of the inheritance of the saints in the light.

52. 2 Thessalanions 2:13
But we are bound to give thanks to God always for you, brethren beloved by the Lord, because God from the beginning chose you for salvation through sanctification by the Spirit and belief in the truth,

53. 1 Timothy 2:1
Therefore I exhort first of all that supplications, prayers, intercessions, and giving of thanks be made for all men,

54. Hebrews 13:5
Let your conduct *be* without covetousness; *be* content with such things as you have. For He Himself has said, "I will never leave you nor forsake you."

55. Revelation 4:9
Whenever the living creatures give glory and honor and thanks to Him who sits on the throne, who lives forever and ever,

56. Revelation 11:17
saying:
"We give You thanks, O Lord God Almighty,
The One who is and who was [a]and who is to come,
Because You have taken Your great power and reigned.

HOUSEHOLD WICKEDNESS

PRAYERS

Let the wickedness of the wicked come to an end in my life in Jesus name.

57.   Matthew 10:36
and 'a man's enemies will be those of his own household.'

58. Genesis 4:8-9
8 Now Cain [a]talked with Abel his [b]brother; and it came to pass, when they were in the field, that Cain rose up against Abel his brother and killed him.
9 Then the Lord said to Cain, "Where is Abel your brother?"
He said, "I do not know. Am I my brother's keeper?"

59. Genesis 37:19-20
19 Then they said to one another, "Look, this dreamer is coming!
20 Come therefore, let us now kill him and cast him into some pit; and we shall say, 'Some wild beast has devoured him.' We shall see what will become of his dreams!"

60. Judges 9:5
Then he went to his father's house at Ophrah and killed his brothers, the seventy sons of Jerubbaal, on one stone. But Jotham the youngest son of Jerubbaal was left, because he hid himself.

61. Judges 9:56-57
56 Thus God repaid the wickedness of Abimelech, which he had done to his father by killing his seventy brothers.

57 And all the evil of the men of Shechem God returned on their own heads, and on them came the curse of Jotham the son of Jerubbaal.

62. Psalm 55:12-14

12 For it is not an enemy who reproaches me;
Then I could bear it.
Nor is it one who hates me who has exalted himself against me;
Then I could hide from him.
13 But it was you, a man my equal,
My companion and my acquaintance.
14 We took sweet counsel together,
And walked to the house of God in the throng.

63. Judges 15:11-13

11 Then three thousand men of Judah went down to the cleft of the rock of Etam, and said to Samson, "Do you not know that the Philistines rule over us? What is this you have done to us?"
And he said to them, "As they did to me, so I have done to them."
12 But they said to him, "We have come down to arrest you, that we may deliver you into the hand of the Philistines." Then Samson said to them, "Swear to me that you will not kill me yourselves."
13 So they spoke to him, saying, "No, but we will tie you securely and deliver you into their hand; but we will surely not kill you." And they bound him with two new ropes and brought him up from the rock.

64. Nahum 3:4-5

4 Because of the multitude of harlotries of the seductive harlot,
The mistress of sorceries,
Who sells nations through her harlotries,

And families through her sorceries.
5 "Behold, I am against you," says the Lord of hosts;
"I will lift your skirts over your face,
I will show the nations your nakedness,
And the kingdoms your shame.

65. Psalm 7:9

Oh, let the wickedness of the wicked come to an end,
But establish the just

66. 2 Chronicles 28:19

For the Lord [a]brought Judah low because of Ahaz king of Israel, for he had encouraged moral decline in Judah and had been continually unfaithful to the Lord.

67. Job 34:26

He strikes them as wicked men
In the open sight of others,

68. Psalm 10:15

Break the arm of the wicked and the evil man;
Seek out his wickedness until You find none.

69. Psalm 45:7

You love righteousness and hate wickedness;
Therefore God, Your God, has anointed You
With the oil of gladness more than Your companions.

70. Psalm 56:7

Shall they escape by iniquity?
In anger cast down the peoples, O God!

71. Psalm 94:23

He has brought on them their own iniquity,
And shall [a]cut them off in their own wickedness;
The Lord our God shall cut them off.

72. Job 24:20
The womb should forget him,
The worm should feed sweetly on him;
He should be remembered no more,
And wickedness should be broken like a tree.

FINANCIAL BREAKTHROUGH

PRAYERS

From today onwards, I receive the power from you to get wealth in Jesus name

73.   Deuteronomy 8:18
But remember the Lord your God, for it is he who gives you the ability to produce wealth, and so confirms his covenant, which he swore to your ancestors, as it is today.

74. Joshua 22:8
saying, "Return to your homes with your great wealth—with large herds of livestock, with silver, gold, bronze and iron, and a great quantity of clothing—and divide the plunder from your enemies with your fellow Israelites."

75. 1 Samuel 2:7
The Lord sends poverty and wealth;
    he humbles and he exalts.

76. 1 Kings 3:13
Moreover, I will give you what you have not asked for—both wealth and honor—so that in your lifetime you will have no equal among kings.

77. 1 Chronicles 29:12
Wealth and honor come from you;
    you are the ruler of all things.
In your hands are strength and power

to exalt and give strength to all.

78. 1 Chronicles 29:28
He died at a good old age, having enjoyed long life, wealth and
honor. His son Solomon succeeded him as king.

79. 2 Chronicles 32:7
"Be strong and courageous. Do not be afraid or discouraged
because of the king of Assyria and the vast army with him, for
there is a greater power with us than with him.

80. Psalm 39:6
"Surely everyone goes around like a mere phantom;
    in vain they rush about, heaping up wealth
    without knowing whose it will finally be.

81. Psalm 45:12

The city of Tyre will come with a gift, people of wealth will seek
your favor.

82. Psalm 112:3
Wealth and riches are in their houses,
    and their righteousness endures forever.

83. Proverbs 6:31
Yet if he is caught, he must pay sevenfold, though it costs him all
the wealth of his house.

84. Proverbs 8:18
With me are riches and honor,
    enduring wealth and prosperity.

85. Proverbs 10:4

   Lazy hands make for poverty,
      but diligent hands bring wealth.

86. Proverbs 10:15

   The wealth of the rich is their fortified city,
      but poverty is the ruin of the poor.

87. Proverbs 10:22

   The blessing of the Lord brings wealth,
      without painful toil for it

88. Proverbs 13:7

   One person pretends to be rich, yet has nothing;
      another pretends to be poor, yet has great wealth.

89. Proverbs 13:22

   A good person leaves an inheritance for their children's children,
      but a sinner's wealth is stored up for the righteous.

90. Proverbs 14:24

   The wealth of the wise is their crown,
      but the folly of fools yields folly.

91. Proverbs 15:16

   Better a little with the fear of the Lord
      than great wealth with turmoil.

92. Proverbs 19:4

   Wealth attracts many friends,
      but even the closest friend of the poor person deserts them.

93. Proverbs 19:14

Houses and wealth are inherited from parents,
    but a prudent wife is from the Lord.

94. Ecclesiastes 2:26

To the person who pleases him, God gives wisdom, knowledge and happiness, but to the sinner he gives the task of gathering and storing up wealth to hand it over to the one who pleases God. This too is meaningless, a chasing after the wind.

95. Ecclesiastes 5:13

I have seen a grievous evil under the sun:
wealth hoarded to the harm of its owners,

96. Ecclesiastes 5:19

Moreover, when God gives someone wealth and possessions, and the ability to enjoy them, to accept their lot and be happy in their toil—this is a gift of God.

DELIVERANCE FROM EVIL

BATTLES

Deliver me from the hands of every evil person in jesus name

97.   Jeremiah 20:11
But the Lord is with me as a mighty, awesome One.
Therefore my persecutors will stumble, and will not prevail.
They will be greatly ashamed, for they will not prosper.
Their everlasting confusion will never be forgotten.

98. Deuteronomy 32:35
Vengeance is Mine, and recompense;
Their foot shall slip in due time;
For the day of their calamity is at hand,
And the things to come hasten upon them.'

99. Deuteronomy 32:36
I said I would scatter them
     and erase their name from human memory,

100.   Psalm 129:2
"they have greatly oppressed me from my youth,
     but they have not gained the victory over me.

101.   Jeremiah 1:19
They will fight against you but will not overcome you, for I am
with you and will rescue you," declares the Lord.

102.   Jeremiah 15:15

O Lord, You know;
Remember me and [a]visit me,
And take vengeance for me on my persecutors.
In Your enduring patience, do not take me away.
Know that for Your sake I have suffered rebuke.

103.   Psalm 65:5

You answer us with awesome and righteous deeds, God our Savior,
the hope of all the ends of the earth and of the farthest seas,

104.   Psalm 66:5

Come and see the works of God;
He is awesome in His doing toward the sons of men.

105.   John 11:44

And he who had died came out bound hand and foot with graveclothes, and his face was wrapped with a cloth. Jesus said to them, "Loose him, and let him go."

106.   Isaiah 49:25-26

25 thus says the Lord:
"Even the captives of the mighty shall be taken away,
And the prey of the terrible be delivered;
For I will contend with him who contends with you,
And I will save your children.
26 I will feed those who oppress you with their own flesh,
And they shall be drunk with their own blood as with sweet wine.
All flesh shall know
That I, the Lord, am your Savior,
And your Redeemer, the Mighty One of Jacob.

107.   Revelation 16:6

For they have spilled the blood of saints and prophets, and You have given them blood to drink, as they deserve.

108.   Psalm 35:1

Contend, Lord, with those who contend with me;
    fight against those who fight against me.

109.   Psalm 46:9

He makes wars cease to the end of the earth;
He breaks the bow and cuts the spear in two;
He burns the chariot in the fire.

110.   Acts 26:17

I will rescue you from your own people and from the Gentiles. I am sending you to them.

111.   Jeremiah 50:27

Slay all her bulls,
Let them go down to the slaughter.
Woe to them!
For their day has come, the time of their punishment.

112.   Psalm 37:13

but the Lord laughs at the wicked,
    for he knows their day is coming.

113.   Proverbs 16:5

Everyone proud in heart is an abomination to the Lord;
Though they join [a]forces, none will go unpunished

114.   Proverbs 16:4

The Lord has made all for Himself,

Yes, even the wicked for the day of doom.

115.   Proverbs 11:21
   Though they join forces, the wicked will not go unpunished;
   But the posterity of the righteous will be delivered.

116.   Proverbs 14:19
   The evil will bow before the good,
   And the wicked at the gates of the righteous.

O' LORD LET MY DEFEATS TURN INTO VICTORIES

117.   Philippians 4:13
I can do all things through [a]Christ who strengthens me.

118.   1 Corinthians 15:57
But thanks be to God! He gives us the victory through our Lord Jesus Christ.

119.   Luke 18:27
But He said, "The things which are impossible with men are possible with God."

120.   1 Corinthians 9:25
And everyone who competes for the prize is temperate in all things. Now they do it to obtain a perishable crown, but we for an imperishable crown.

121.   James 1:12
Blessed is the man who endures temptation; for when he has been approved, he will receive the crown of life which the Lord has promised to those who love Him.

122.   2 Timothy 4:8

Now there is in store for me the crown of righteousness, which the Lord, the righteous Judge, will award to me on that day—and not only to me, but also to all who have longed for his appearing.

123.   1 Peter 5:4
And when the Chief Shepherd appears, you will receive the crown of glory that will never fade away.

124.   1 Thessalonians 2:19
For what is our hope, or joy, or crown of rejoicing? Is it not even you in the presence of our Lord Jesus Christ at His coming?

125.   Matthew 20:16
"So the last will be first, and the first will be last."

126.   1 Corinthians 9:24
Do you not know that those who run in a race all run, but one receives the prize? Run in such a way that you may obtain it.

127.   1 John 5:4
for everyone born of God overcomes the world. This is the victory that has overcome the world, even our faith.

128.   Daniel 12:3
Those who are wise will shine like the brightness of the heavens, and those who lead many to righteousness, like the stars for ever and ever.

129.   Deuteronomy 20:4

For the Lord your God is the one who goes with you to fight for you against your enemies to give you victory."

130.   Galatians 6:9

Let us not become weary in doing good, for at the proper time we will reap a harvest if we do not give up.

131.   Hebrews 12:1

Therefore, since we are surrounded by such a great cloud of witnesses, let us throw off everything that hinders and the sin that so easily entangles. And let us run with perseverance the race marked out for us,

132.   Psalm 37:23-24

23 The Lord makes firm the steps
    of the one who delights in him;
24 though he may stumble, he will not fall,
    for the Lord upholds him with his hand.

133.   Isaiah 40:31

but those who hope in the Lord
    will renew their strength.
They will soar on wings like eagles;
    they will run and not grow weary,
    they will walk and not be faint.

134.   Nehemiah 8:10

Nehemiah said, "Go and enjoy choice food and sweet drinks, and send some to those who have nothing prepared. This day is holy to our Lord. Do not grieve, for the joy of the Lord is your strength."

BREAKTHROUGH IS AT YOUR GATES

I am entering my gates of break through and promotion by fire and by force.

135.   Genesis 22:17

I will surely bless you and make your descendants as numerous as the stars in the sky and as the sand on the seashore. Your descendants will take possession of the cities of their enemies,

136.   Isaiah 60:18

No longer will violence be heard in your land,
    nor ruin or destruction within your borders,
but you will call your walls Salvation
    and your gates Praise.

137.   Matthew 16:18

And I tell you that you are Peter,and on this rock I will build my church, and the gates of Hades will not overcome it.

138.   Nehemiah 2:13

And I went out by night through the Valley Gate to the Serpent Well and the Refuse Gate, and viewed the walls of Jerusalem which were broken down and its gates which were burned with fire.

139.   Nehemiah 2:14

Then I moved on toward the Fountain Gate and the King's Pool, but there was not enough room for my mount to get through;

140.   Nehemiah 3:26

and the temple servants living on the hill of Ophel made repairs up to a point opposite the Water Gate toward the east and the projecting tower.

141.   Nehemiah 3:1

Eliashib the high priest and his fellow priests went to work and rebuilt the Sheep Gate. They dedicated it and set its doors in place, building as far as the Tower of the Hundred, which they dedicated, and as far as the Tower of Hananel.

142.   Joel 2:28

"And afterward,
    I will pour out my Spirit on all people.
Your sons and daughters will prophesy,
    your old men will dream dreams,
    your young men will see visions

143.   Ezekiel 47:1-5

The man brought me back to the entrance to the temple, and I saw water coming out from under the threshold of the temple toward the east (for the temple faced east). The water was coming down from under the south side of the temple, south of the altar.

2 He then brought me out through the north gate and led me around the outside to the outer gate facing east, and the water was trickling from the south side.

3 As the man went eastward with a measuring line in his hand, he measured off a thousand cubits and then led me through water that was ankle-deep.

4 He measured off another thousand cubits and led me through water that was knee-deep. He measured off another thousand and led me through water that was up to the waist.

5 He measured off another thousand, but now it was a river that I could not cross, because the water had risen and was deep enough to swim in—a river that no one could cross.

144.   Isaiah 60:11

Your gates will always stand open, they will never be shut, day or night,
so that people may bring you the wealth of the nations—
    their kings led in triumphal procession.

145.   Genesis 28:17

He was afraid and said, "How awesome is this place! This is none other than the house of God; this is the gate of heaven."

146.   Lamentations 5:14

The elders are gone from the city gate;
    the young men have stopped their music.

Break Through Prayers Against Stubborn Enemies

All stubborn enemies will be crushed by the rock of ages and will rise no more.

147.   Isaiah 14:25
I will crush the Assyrian in my land;
   on my mountains I will trample him down.
His yoke will be taken from my people,
   and his burden removed from their shoulders.

148.   Isaiah 45:2
I will go before you
   and will level the mountains;
I will break down gates of bronze
   and cut through bars of iron.

149.   Psalm 2:9
You shall [a]break them with a rod of iron;
You shall dash them to pieces like a potter's vessel.

150.   Psalm 10:15
Break the arm of the wicked and the evil man;
Seek out his wickedness until You find none.

151.   Psalm 58:6
Break the teeth in their mouths, O God; Lord, tear out the fangs of those lions!

152.   Psalm 72:4

He will bring justice to the poor of the people;
He will save the children of the needy,
And will break in pieces the oppressor.

153.   Daniel 8:8

The goat became very great, but at the height of its power the large horn was broken off, and in its place four prominent horns grew up toward the four winds of heaven.

154.   Daniel 11:4

And when he has arisen, his kingdom shall be broken up and divided toward the four winds of heaven, but not among his posterity nor according to his dominion with which he ruled; for his kingdom shall be uprooted, even for others besides these.

155.   Ezekiel 30:4

A sword will come against Egypt,
    and anguish will come upon Cush.
When the slain fall in Egypt,
    her wealth will be carried away
    and her foundations torn down.

156.   Psalm 37:14

The wicked have drawn the sword
And have bent their bow,
To cast down the poor and needy,
To slay those who are of upright conduct.

157.   Jeremiah 51:21

with you I shatter horse and rider,
with you I shatter chariot and driver,

158.	Jeremiah 23:29
"Is not my word like fire," declares the Lord, "and like a hammer that breaks a rock in pieces?

159.	Ezekiel 13:14
So I will break down the wall you have plastered with untempered mortar, and bring it down to the ground, so that its foundation will be uncovered; it will fall, and you shall be consumed in the midst of it. Then you shall know that I am the Lord.

160.	Hosea 10:2
Their heart is deceitful,
and now they must bear their guilt.
The Lord will demolish their altars
and destroy their sacred stones.

161.	Deuteronomy 7:5
But thus you shall deal with them: you shall destroy their altars, and break down their sacred pillars, and cut down their wooden images, and burn their carved images with fire.

162.	Isaiah 28:18
Your covenant with death will be annulled; your agreement with the realm of the dead will not stand. When the overwhelming scourge sweeps by, you will be beaten down by it.

WARFARE PRAYERS

BATTLE AT THE GATES

Lord I build you an alter, where angels can assend and descend and bring victory.

163.   Genesis 22:17

blessing I will bless you, and multiplying I will multiply your descendants as the stars of the heaven and as the sand which is on the seashore; and your descendants shall possess the gate of their enemies.

164.   Genesis 26:60

And they blessed Rebekah and said to her:
"Our sister, may you become
The mother of thousands of ten thousands;
And may your descendants possess
The gates of those who hate them."

165.   Isaiah 45:1-3

1 "Thus says the Lord to His anointed,
To Cyrus, whose right hand I have held—
To subdue nations before him
And loose the armor of kings,
To open before him the double doors,
So that the gates will not be shut:
2 'I will go before you
And make the crooked places straight;
I will break in pieces the gates of bronze
And cut the bars of iron.

3 I will give you the treasures of darkness
And hidden riches of secret places,
That you may know that I, the Lord,
Who call you by your name,
Am the God of Israel.

166.　　　Zechariah 9:11-12
11 "As for you also,
Because of the blood of your covenant,
I will set your prisoners free from the waterless pit.
12 Return to the stronghold,
You prisoners of hope.
Even today I declare
That I will restore double to you

167.　　　Acts 12:10
When they were past the first and the second guard posts, they came to the iron gate that leads to the city, which opened to them of its own accord; and they went out and went down one street, and immediately the angel departed from him.

168.　　　Acts 16:26
Suddenly there was a great earthquake, so that the foundations of the prison were shaken; and immediately all the doors were opened and everyone's chains were loosed.

169.　　　Joshua 6:1
Now Jericho was securely shut up because of the children of Israel; none went out, and none came in.

170.　　　Isaiah 60:11
Therefore your gates shall be open continually;

They shall not be shut day or night,
That men may bring to you the wealth of the Gentiles,
And their kings in procession.

171.   Matthew 16:18

And I also say to you that you are Peter, and on this rock I will
build My church, and the gates of Hades shall not prevail against
it.

172.   Psalm 129:2

Many a time they have afflicted me from my youth;
Yet they have not prevailed against me.

173.   Hebrews 11:33-34

33 who through faith subdued kingdoms, worked righteousness,
obtained promises, stopped the mouths of lions,
34 quenched the violence of fire, escaped the edge of the sword,
out of weakness were made strong, became valiant in battle,
turned to flight the armies of the aliens.

DELIVERANCE FROM

THE HAND OF THE WICKED

Let every evil hand stealing my blessing wither by fire in Jesus name

174.   Ephesians 6:13
Therefore take up the whole armor of God, that you may be able to withstand in the evil day, and having done all, to stand.

175.   2 Timothy 4:18
And the Lord will deliver me from every evil work and preserve me for His heavenly kingdom. To Him be glory forever and ever. Amen!

176.   John 17:15
I do not pray that You should take them out of the world, but that You should keep them from the evil one.

177.   Psalm 71:4
Deliver me, O my God, out of the hand of the wicked,
Out of the hand of the unrighteous and cruel man.

178.   Jeremiah 15:20-21
20 And I will make you to this people a fortified bronze wall;
And they will fight against you,
But they shall not prevail against you;
For I am with you to save you
And deliver you," says the Lord.
21 I will deliver you from the hand of the wicked,

And I will redeem you from the grip of the terrible.

179.   Psalm 140:1

Deliver me, O Lord, from evil men; Preserve me from violent men,

180.   Psalm 72:8

He shall have dominion also from sea to sea, And from the River to the ends of the earth.

181.   Obadiah 1:17

But on Mount Zion there shall be deliverance,
And there shall be holiness;
The house of Jacob shall possess their possessions.

182.   Psalm 75:10

"All the horns of the wicked I will also cut off,
But the horns of the righteous shall be exalted."

183.   Zechariah 1:21

And I said, "What are these coming to do?"
So he said, "These are the horns that scattered Judah, so that no one could lift up his head; but the craftsmen are coming to terrify them, to cast out the horns of the nations that lifted up their horn against the land of Judah to scatter it."

184.   Psalm 51:14

Deliver me from the guilt of bloodshed, O God,
The God of my salvation,
And my tongue shall sing aloud of Your righteousness.

185.   Zechariah 9:11

As for you also, Because of the blood of your covenant, I will set
your prisoners free from the waterless pit.

LET GOD

ARISE PRAYERS

Lord, arise to your rest and dwell within our Praise.

186.   Psalm 68:1-3
1 Let God arise,
Let His enemies be scattered;
Let those also who hate Him flee before Him.
2 As smoke is driven away,
So drive them away;
As wax melts before the fire,
So let the wicked perish at the presence of God.
3 But let the righteous be glad;
Let them rejoice before God;
Yes, let them rejoice exceedingly.

187.   Psalm 3:7
Arise, O Lord;
Save me, O my God!
For You have struck all my enemies on the cheekbone;
You have broken the teeth of the ungodly

.

188.   Psalm 7:6
Arise, O Lord, in Your anger;
Lift Yourself up because of the rage of my enemies;
Rise up for me to the judgment You have commanded!

189.   Psalm 9:19

Arise, O Lord,
Do not let man prevail;
Let the nations be judged in Your sight.

190.   Psalm 12:5

"For the oppression of the poor, for the sighing of the needy,
Now I will arise," says the Lord;
"I will set him in the safety for which he yearns."

191.   Psalm 17:13

Arise, O Lord,
Confront him, cast him down;
Deliver my life from the wicked with Your sword,

192.   Psalm 35:4-5

4 Let those be put to shame and brought to dishonor
Who seek after my life;
Let those be turned back and brought to confusion
Who plot my hurt.
5 Let them be like chaff before the wind,
And let the angel of the Lord chase them.

193.   Psalm 107:2

Let the redeemed of the Lord say so,
Whom He has redeemed from the hand of the enemy,

194.   Psalm 83:17

Let them be confounded and dismayed forever;
Yes, let them be put to shame and perish,

195.   Psalm 109:29

Let my accusers be clothed with shame,
And let them cover themselves with their own disgrace as with a
mantle.

196.   Psalm 129:5
Let all those who hate Zion
Be put to shame and turned back.

197.   Psalm 70:2
Let them be ashamed and confounded
Who seek my life;
Let them be turned back and confused
Who desire my hurt.

198.   Jeremiah 20:11
But the Lord is with me as a mighty, awesome One.
Therefore my persecutors will stumble, and will not prevail.
They will be greatly ashamed, for they will not prosper.
Their everlasting confusion will never be forgotten.

199.   John 11:44
And he who had died came out bound hand and foot with
graveclothes, and his face was wrapped with a cloth. Jesus said
to them, "Loose him, and let him go."

200.   Isaiah 49:25-26
25 But thus says the Lord:
"Even the captives of the mighty shall be taken away,
And the prey of the terrible be delivered;
For I will contend with him who contends with you,
And I will save your children.
26 I will feed those who oppress you with their own flesh,

And they shall be drunk with their own blood as with sweet wine.
All flesh shall know
That I, the Lord, am your Savior,
And your Redeemer, the Mighty One of Jacob. "

201.   Psalm 102:13
You will arise and have mercy on Zion;
For the time to favor her,
Yes, the set time, has come.

My Divine Escape.

I will Escape

This year I will escape every demonic, trap, snare or pit the enemy has prepared. Let him fall into the pit which he has dug. Let the snare be broken.

202.   Psalm 34:4
I sought the Lord, and He heard me,
And delivered me from all my fears.

203.   Psalm 32:7
You are my hiding place;
You shall preserve me from trouble;
You shall surround me with songs of deliverance. Selah

204.   Psalm 124:7
Our soul has escaped as a bird from the snare of the fowlers;
The snare is broken, and we have escaped.

205.   Exodus 23:28
And I will send hornets before you, which shall drive out the Hivite, the Canaanite, and the Hittite from before you.

206.   Genesis 7:7
So Noah, with his sons, his wife, and his sons' wives, went into the ark because of the waters of the flood.

207.   1 Samuel 23:28

Therefore Saul returned from pursuing David, and went against the Philistines; so they called that place the Rock of Escape.

208.   Job 11:20
But the eyes of the wicked will fail,
And they shall not escape,
And their hope - loss of life!

209.   Psalm 55:8
I would hasten my escape
From the windy storm and tempest."

210.   Psalm 141:10
Let the wicked fall into their own nets,
While I escape safely.

211.   Proverbs 19:5
Laziness casts one into a deep sleep,
And an idle person will suffer hunger.

212.   Ecclesiastes 7:18
It is good that you grasp this,
And also not remove your hand from the other;
For he who fears God will escape them all.

213.   2 Timothy 2:26
and that they may come to their senses and escape the snare of the devil, having been taken captive by him to do his will.

214.   Romans 8:35

Who shall separate us from the love of Christ? Shall tribulation, or distress, or persecution, or famine, or nakedness, or peril, or sword?

215.   Psalm 3:3
But You, O Lord, are a shield for me,
My glory and the One who lifts up my head

216.   Jeremiah 15:21
I will deliver you from the hand of the wicked,
And I will redeem you from the grip of the terrible.

217.   Psalm 102:19-20
19 For He looked down from the height of His sanctuary;
From heaven the Lord viewed the earth,
20 To hear the groaning of the prisoner,
To release those appointed to death,

ESTABLISHING GOD'S NAME
FOREVER PRAYERS

A t your name, let every demonic force fighting the church
Bow now IJN

218.   Genesis 3:22
*Then the Lord God said, "Behold, the man has become like
one of Us, to know good and evil. And now, lest he put out
his hand and take also of the tree of life, and eat, and live
forever"—*

219.   Genesis 13:15
*for all the land which you see I give to you and your descendants
forever.*

220.   Exodus 15:18
"The Lord shall reign forever and ever."

221.   2 Samuel 7:13
He shall build a house for My name, and I will establish the throne
of his kingdom forever.

222.   2 Samuel 7:26
So let Your name be magnified forever, saying, 'The Lord of
hosts is the God over Israel.' And let the house of Your servant
David be established before You.

223.   1 Kings 9:3
And the Lord said to him: "I have heard your prayer and your
supplication that you have made before Me; I have consecrated

this house which you have built to put My name there forever, and My eyes and My heart will be there perpetually.

224.   1 Chronicles 16:14-15
14 He is the Lord our God;
His judgments are in all the earth.
15 Remember His covenant forever,
The word which He commanded, for a thousand generations,

225.   Job 36:7
He does not withdraw His eyes from the righteous; But they are on the throne with kings, For He has seated them forever, And they are exalted.

226.   Psalm 149:9
To execute on them the written judgment—
This honor have all His saints.

227.   Psalm 9:5
You have rebuked the nations,
You have destroyed the wicked;
You have blotted out their name forever and ever.

228.   Psalm 9:18
For the needy shall not always be forgotten;
The expectation of the poor shall not perish forever.

229.   Psalm 10:16
The Lord is King forever and ever;
The nations have perished out of His land.

230.   Psalm 23:6

Surely goodness and mercy shall follow me
All the days of my life;
And I will dwell in the house of the Lord Forever.

231.　　　Psalm 33:11

The counsel of the Lord stands forever,
The plans of His heart to all generations.

232.　　　Psalm 37:28

For the Lord loves justice,
And does not forsake His saints;
They are preserved forever,
But the descendants of the wicked shall be cut off

233.　　　Psalm 45:6

Your throne, O God, is forever and ever;
A scepter of righteousness is the scepter of Your kingdom.

234.　　　Psalm 45:17

I will make Your name to be remembered in all generations;
Therefore the people shall praise You forever and ever.

235.　　　Psalm 48:14

For this is God,
Our God forever and ever;
He will be our guide
Even to death.

236.　　　Psalm 73:26

My flesh and my heart fail;
But God is the strength of my heart and my portion forever.

237.   Psalm 93:5
Your testimonies are very sure;
Holiness adorns Your house,
O Lord, forever.

238.   Psalm 110:4
The Lord has sworn
And will not relent,
"You are a priest forever
According to the order of Melchizedek."

239.   Psalm 111:3
His work is honorable and glorious,
And His righteousness endures forever.

240.   Psalm 117:2
For His merciful kindness is great toward us,
And the truth of the Lord endures forever.
Praise the Lord!

241.   Psalm 145:1
I will extol You, my God, O King;
And I will bless Your name forever and ever.

242.   Isaiah 40:8
The grass withers, the flower fades,
But the word of our God stands forever."

243.   Psalm 119:89
Forever, O Lord,
Your word is settled in heaven.

244.   1 Kings 5:3

You know how my father David could not build a house for the name of the Lord his God because of the wars which were fought against him on every side, until the Lord put his foes under the soles of his feet.

PRAYERS TO PUT THE ENEMY UNDER YOUR FEET

From this day going forward, let my enemies become my footstool

245.   1 Kings 5:3-4

3 You know how my father David could not build a house for the name of the Lord his God because of the wars which were fought against him on every side, until the Lord put his foes under the soles of his feet.

4 But now the Lord my God has given me rest on every side; there is neither adversary nor evil occurrence.

246.   Genesis 14:20

And blessed be God Most High, Who has delivered your enemies into your hand." And he gave him a tithe of all.

247.   Genesis 22:17

blessing I will bless you, and multiplying I will multiply your descendants as the stars of the heaven and as the sand which is on the seashore; and your descendants shall possess the gate of their enemies.

248.   Genesis 49:8

"Judah, you are he whom your brothers shall praise; Your hand shall be on the neck of your enemies; Your father's children shall bow down before you.

249.   Exodus 23:22

If you listen carefully to what he says and do all that I say, I will be an enemy to your enemies and will oppose those who oppose you

250.   Exodus 23:27

"I will send My fear before you, I will cause confusion among all the people to whom you come, and will make all your enemies turn their backs to you.

251.   Leviticus 26:7-8

7   *You will chase your enemies, and they shall fall by the sword before you.*

8   *Five of you shall chase a hundred, and a hundred of you shall put ten thousand to flight; your enemies shall fall by the sword before you.*

252.   Numbers 10:35

So it was, whenever the ark set out, that Moses said: "Rise up, O Lord! Let Your enemies be scattered, And let those who hate You flee before You."

253.   Deuteronomy 12:10

But when you cross over the Jordan and dwell in the land which the Lord your God is giving you to inherit, and He gives you rest from all your enemies round about, so that you dwell in safety,

254.   Deuteronomy 23:9

"When the army goes out against your enemies, then keep yourself from every wicked thing."

255.   Deuteronomy 23:14

For the Lord your God walks in the midst of your camp, to deliver you and give your enemies over to you; therefore your camp shall be holy, that He may see no unclean thing among you, and turn away from you.

256.   Deuteronomy 20:4

for the Lord your God is He who goes with you, to fight for you against your enemies, to save you.'

257.   Deuteronomy 21:10

"When you go out to war against your enemies, and the Lord your God delivers them into your hand, and you take them captive,

258.   Deuteronomy 20:14

But the women, the little ones, the livestock, and all that is in the city, all its spoil, you shall plunder for yourself; and you shall eat the enemies' plunder which the Lord your God gives you.

259.   Deuteronomy 25:19

Therefore it shall be, when the Lord your God has given you rest from your enemies all around, in the land which the Lord your God is giving you to possess as an inheritance, that you will blot out the remembrance of Amalek from under heaven. You shall not forget.

260.   Deuteronomy 28:7

"The Lord will cause your enemies who rise against you to be defeated before your face; they shall come out against you one way and flee before you seven ways.

261.   Judges 5:31

"Thus let all Your enemies perish, O Lord! But let those who love Him be like the sun When it comes out in full strength." So the land had rest for forty years.

262. 1 Samuel 25:26

Now therefore, my lord, as the Lord lives and as your soul lives, since the Lord has held you back from coming to bloodshed and from avenging[a] yourself with your own hand, now then, let your enemies and those who seek harm for my lord be as Nabal.

263. 1 Chronicles 14:19

So they went up to Baal Perazim, and David defeated them there. Then David said, "God has broken through my enemies by my hand like a breakthrough of water." Therefore they called the name of that place Baal Perazim.

264. 1 Chronicles 22:9

Behold, a son shall be born to you, who shall be a man of rest; and I will give him rest from all his enemies all around. His name shall be [a]Solomon, for I will give peace and quietness to Israel in his days.

265. Nehemiah 4:15

And I looked, and arose and said to the nobles, to the leaders, and to the rest of the people, "Do not be afraid of them. Remember the Lord, great and awesome, and fight for your brethren, your sons, your daughters, your wives, and your houses."

266. Nehemiah 6:16

And it happened, when all our enemies heard of it, and all the nations around us saw these things, that they were very disheartened in their own eyes; for they perceived that this work was done by our God.

267.   Esther 9:11
On that day the number of those who were killed in Shushan the citadel was brought to the king.

268.   Psalm 3:7
Arise, O Lord; Save me, O my God! For You have struck all my enemies on the cheekbone; You have broken the teeth of the ungodly.

269.   2 Chronicles 20:29
The fear of God came on all the surrounding kingdoms when they heard how the Lord had fought against the enemies of Israel.

PRAYERS TO STOP PATTERNS OF EVIL OCCURRENCE

Let every evil pattern and cycle, affecting my destiny be broken

270.   1 Kings 5:3-4
3 You know how my father David could not build a house for the name of the Lord his God because of the wars which were fought against him on every side, until the Lord put his foes under the soles of his feet.
4 But now the Lord my God has given me rest on every side; there is neither adversary nor evil occurrence.

271.   Genesis 44:4
When they had gone out of the city, and were not yet far off, Joseph said to his steward, "Get up, follow the men; and when you overtake them, say to them, 'Why have you repaid evil for good?

272.   Genesis 50:20
But as for you, you meant evil against me; but God meant it for good, in order to bring it about as it is this day, to save many people alive.

273.   Exodus 10:10
Then he said to them, "The Lord had better be with you when I let you and your little ones go! Beware, for evil is ahead of you.

274.   1 Samuel 23:9
When David knew that Saul plotted evil against him, he said to Abiathar the priest, "Bring the ephod here."

275.　　　1 Samuel 25:3

The name of the man was Nabal, and the name of his wife Abigail. And she was a woman of good understanding and beautiful appearance; but the man was harsh and evil in his doings. He was of the house of Caleb.

276.　　　1 Kings 13:33

After this event Jeroboam did not turn from his evil way, but again he made priests from every class of people for the high places; whoever wished, he consecrated him, and he became one of the priests of the high places.

277.　　　Nehemiah 6:13

For this reason he was hired, that I should be afraid and act that way and sin, so that they might have cause for an evil report, that they might reproach me.

278.　　　Nehemiah 9:28

"But after they had rest,
They again did evil before You.
Therefore You left them in the hand of their enemies,
So that they had dominion over them;
Yet when they returned and cried out to You,
You heard from heaven;
And many times You delivered them according to Your mercies,

279.　　　Esther 8:3

Now Esther spoke again to the king, fell down at his feet, and implored him with tears to counteract the evil of Haman the Agagite, and the scheme which he had devised against the Jews.

280.   Job 5:19

He shall deliver you in six troubles,
Yes, in seven no evil shall touch you.

281.   Job 30:26

But when I looked for good, evil came to me;
And when I waited for light, then came darkness.

282.   Psalm 5:4

For You are not a God who takes pleasure in wickedness,
Nor shall evil dwell with You.

283.   Psalm 34:21

Evil shall slay the wicked,
And those who hate the righteous shall be condemned.

284.   Psalm 37:19

They shall not be ashamed in the evil time,
And in the days of famine they shall be satisfied.

285.   Psalm 54:5

He will repay my enemies for their evil.
Cut them off in Your truth

286.   Psalm 64:5

They encourage themselves in an evil matter;
They talk of laying snares secretly;
They say, "Who will see them?"

287.   Psalm 64:7

But God shall shoot at them with an arrow;
Suddenly they shall be wounded.

288.   Psalm 91:10
No evil shall befall you,
Nor shall any plague come near your dwelling;

289.   Psalm 109:18-20
18 As he clothed himself with cursing as with his garment,
So let it enter his body like water,
And like oil into his bones.
19 Let it be to him like the garment which covers him,
And for a belt with which he girds himself continually.
20 Let this be the Lord's reward to my accusers,
And to those who speak evil against my person.

290.   Psalm 119:101
I have restrained my feet from every evil way,
That I may keep Your word.

291.   Psalm 121:7
The Lord shall preserve you from all evil;
He shall preserve your soul.

292.   Psalm 140:1-2
1 Deliver me, O Lord, from evil men;
Preserve me from violent men,
2 Who plan evil things in their hearts;
They continually gather together for war.

293.   Proverbs 6:24
To keep you from the evil woman,
From the flattering tongue of a seductress.

294.   Proverbs 11:9
The hypocrite with his mouth destroys his neighbor,
But through knowledge the righteous will be delivered.

295.   Proverbs 13:21
Evil pursues sinners,
But to the righteous, good shall be repaid.

296.   Proverbs 14:19
The evil will bow before the good,
And the wicked at the gates of the righteous.

297.   Proverbs 15:3
The eyes of the Lord are in every place,
Keeping watch on the evil and the good.

298.   Proverbs 17:11
An evil man seeks only rebellion;
Therefore a cruel messenger will be sent against him.

299.   Nahum 1:5
Look, there on the mountains, the feet of one who brings good
news, who proclaims peace! Celebrate your festivals, O Judah,
and fulfill your vows. No more will the wicked invade you; they
will be completely destroyed.

Dealing with Animalistic Spirits Prayers

I trample over scorpions and serpents and every animalistic spirit fighting against my life.

300.   Genesis 1:20-22

20 Then God said, "Let the waters abound with an abundance of living creatures, and let birds fly above the earth across the face of the firmament of the heavens."
21 So God created great sea creatures and every living thing that moves, with which the waters abounded, according to their kind, and every winged bird according to its kind. And God saw that it was good.
22 And God blessed them, saying, "Be fruitful and multiply, and fill the waters in the seas, and let birds multiply on the earth."

301.   Genesis 2:19-20

19 Out of the ground the Lord God formed every beast of the field and every bird of the air, and brought them to Adam to see what he would call them. And whatever Adam called each living creature, that was its name.
20 So Adam gave names to all cattle, to the birds of the air, and to every beast of the field. But for Adam there was not found a helper comparable to him.

302.   Genesis 3:1

Now the serpent was more cunning than any beast of the field which the Lord God had made. And he said to the woman, "Has God indeed said, 'You shall not eat of every tree of the garden'?"

303.	Genesis 3:21

Also for Adam and his wife the Lord God made tunics of skin, and clothed them.

304.	Genesis 4:4

Abel also brought of the firstborn of his flock and of their fat. And the Lord respected Abel and his offering,

305.	Genesis 7:1

Then the Lord said to Noah, "Come into the ark, you and all your household, because I have seen that you are righteous before Me in this generation.

306.	Genesis 14:20

And blessed be God Most High, Who has delivered your enemies into your hand." And he gave him a tithe of all.

307.	Revelation 18:2

And he cried mightily with a loud voice, saying, "Babylon the great is fallen, is fallen, and has become a dwelling place of demons, a prison for every foul spirit, and a cage for every unclean and hated bird!

308.	Genesis 15:11

And when the vultures came down on the carcasses, Abram drove them away.

309.	Genesis 40:17-19

17 In the uppermost basket were all kinds of baked goods for Pharaoh, and the birds ate them out of the basket on my head."
18 So Joseph answered and said, "This is the interpretation of it: The three baskets are three days.

19 Within three days Pharaoh will lift off your head from you and hang you on a tree; and the birds will eat your flesh from you."

310.   Isaiah 34:11

That the vomiting pelican and the bittern may possess it: And the great owl and the raven, dwell therein; Then will he stretch out over it The line of desolation, and The plummet of emptiness.

Prayers to Stop the Agenda of Evil Birds

I decree that every evil bird and monitoring spirits be blinded in Jesus name.

311.   Luke 10:19

Behold, I give you the authority to trample on serpents and scorpions, and over all the power of the enemy, and nothing shall by any means hurt you.

312.   Psalm 91:13

You will tread on the lion and the cobra;
  you will trample the great lion and the serpent.

313.   Mark 16:18

they will take up serpents; and if they drink anything deadly, it will by no means hurt them; they will lay hands on the sick, and they will recover."

314.   Isaiah 34:11

That the vomiting pelican and the bittern may possess it: And the great owl and the raven, dwell therein; Then will he stretch out over it The line of desolation, and The plummet of emptiness.

315.   Micah 1:8

Because of this I will weep and wail;
  I will go about barefoot and naked.
I will howl like a jackal
  and moan like an owl.

316.   Genesis 8:7

Then he sent out a raven, which kept going to and fro until the waters had dried up from the earth.

317.   Hosea 8:1

"Set the trumpet to your mouth!
He shall come like an eagle against the house of the Lord,
Because they have transgressed My covenant
And rebelled against My law.

318.   Jeremiah 49:22

Behold, He shall come up and fly like the eagle,
And spread His wings over Bozrah;
The heart of the mighty men of Edom in that day shall be
Like the heart of a woman in birth pangs.

319.   Jeremiah 12:9

My heritage is to Me like a speckled vulture;
The vultures all around are against her.
Come, assemble all the beasts of the field,
Bring them to devour!

320.   Leviticus 12:6

'When the days of her purification are fulfilled, whether for a son or a daughter, she shall bring to the priest a lamb of the first year as a burnt offering, and a young pigeon or a turtledove as a sin offering, to the door of the tabernacle of meeting.

321.   2 Samuel 21:10

Now Rizpah the daughter of Aiah took sackcloth and spread it for herself on the rock, from the beginning of harvest until the late rains poured on them from heaven. And she did not allow the birds of the air to rest on them by day nor the beasts of the field by night.

322.   Revelation 18:2

And he cried mightily with a loud voice, saying, "Babylon the great is fallen, is fallen, and has become a dwelling place of demons, a prison for every foul spirit, and a cage for every unclean and hated bird!

323.   Psalm 8:7-8

7 All sheep and oxen—
Even the beasts of the field,
8 The birds of the air,
And the fish of the sea
That pass through the paths of the seas

324.   Ecclesiastes 9:12

For man also does not know his time:
Like fish taken in a cruel net,
Like birds caught in a snare,
So the sons of men are snared in an evil time,
When it falls suddenly upon them.

325.   Job 39:26-30

26 "Does the hawk take flight by your wisdom
   and spread its wings toward the south?
27 Does the eagle soar at your command
   and build its nest on high?
28 It dwells on a cliff and stays there at night;
   a rocky crag is its stronghold.
29 From there it looks for food;

its eyes detect it from afar.
30 Its young ones feast on blood,
    and where the slain are, there it is."

326.   Jeremiah 5:27
As a cage is full of birds,
So their houses are full of deceit.
Therefore they have become great and grown rich.

327.   Isaiah 16:2
Above him were seraphim, each with six wings: With two wings
they covered their faces, with two they covered their feet, and with
two they were flying.

328.   Jeremiah 4:25-26
25 I beheld, and indeed there was no man,
And all the birds of the heavens had fled.
26 I beheld, and indeed the fruitful land was a wilderness,
And all its cities were broken down
At the presence of the Lord,
By His fierce anger.

329.   Zephaniah 1:3
"I will consume man and beast;
I will consume the birds of the heavens,
The fish of the sea,
And the stumbling blocks along with the wicked.
I will cut off man from the face of the land,"
Says the Lord.

330.   Psalm 91:14

"Because he has set his love upon Me, therefore I will deliver him;
I will set him on high, because he has known My name.

331.   Job 30:29
I am a brother of jackals,
And a companion of ostriches.

332.   Jeremiah 9:10
Who doeth great things past finding out, and wonders without number.

DELIVERANCE FROM ANIMALISTIC SPIRITUAL ATTACKS

I cancel every sudden attack, every planned attack and every attack in the womb of my tomorrow that will make me miscarry my blessings. I will carry full term in Jesus name.

333.   Luke 10:19

Behold, I give you the authority to trample on serpents and scorpions, and over all the power of the enemy, and nothing shall by any means hurt you.

334.   Psalm 91:13

You will tread on the lion and the cobra;
*   you will trample the great lion and the serpent.*

335.   Mark 16:18

they will take up serpents; and if they drink anything deadly, it will by no means hurt them; they will lay hands on the sick, and they will recover."

336.   Revelation 16:13

And I saw three unclean spirits like frogs coming out of the mouth of the dragon, out of the mouth of the beast, and out of the mouth of the false prophet.

337.   Psalm 118:12

They swarmed around me like bees,
*   but they were consumed as quickly as burning thorns;*
*   in the name of the Lord I cut them down.*

338.   Deuteronomy 1:44

And the Amorites who dwelt in that mountain came out against you and chased you as bees do, and drove you back from Seir to Hormah.

339.   Daniel 7:5

"And there before me was a second beast, which looked like a bear. It was raised up on one of its sides, and it had three ribs in its mouth between its teeth. It was told, 'Get up and eat your fill of flesh!'

340.   Psalm 7:2

or they will tear me apart like a lion
     and rip me to pieces with no one to rescue me. (nkjv)

lest like a lion they tear my soul apart, rending it in pieces, with none to deliver. (esv)

341.   Psalm 58:6

Break the teeth in their mouths, O God;
     Lord, tear out the fangs of those lions!

342.   Exodus 7:12

For every man threw down his rod, and they became serpents. But Aaron's rod swallowed up their rods.

343.   2 Corinthians 11:3

But I fear, lest somehow, as the serpent deceived Eve by his craftiness, so your minds may be corrupted from the simplicity that is in Christ.

344.   Isaiah 14:29

"Do not rejoice, all you of Philistia,
Because the rod that struck you is broken;
For out of the serpent's roots will come forth a viper,
And its offspring will be a fiery flying serpent.

345.   Ecclesiastes 10:19
Dead flies putrefy the perfumer's ointment,
And cause it to give off a foul odor;
So does a little folly to one respected for wisdom and honor.

346.   Psalm 78:45
He sent divers sorts of flies among them, which devoured them;
and frogs, which destroyed them.

347.   Isaiah 34:14
The wild beasts of the desert shall also meet with the [a]jackals,
And the wild goat shall bleat to its companion;
Also the night creature shall rest there,
And find for herself a place of rest.

348.   Habakkuk 1:8
Their horses also are swifter than leopards,
And more fierce than evening wolves.
Their chargers charge ahead;
Their cavalry comes from afar;
They fly as the eagle that hastens to eat.

349.   Psalm 42:1
As the deer pants for the water brooks,
So pants my soul for You, O God.

350.   Psalm 18:33

He makes my feet like the feet of deer,
And sets me on my high places.

351.   Psalm 22:16
For dogs have surrounded Me;
The congregation of the wicked has enclosed Me.
They pierced My hands and My feet;

352.   Exodus 11:7
But against none of the children of Israel shall a dog [a]move its
tongue, against man or beast, that you may know that the Lord
does make a difference between the Egyptians and Israel.'

353.   Psalm 22:12-13
12 Many bulls have surrounded Me;
Strong bulls of Bashan have encircled Me.
13 They gape at Me with their mouths,
Like a raging and roaring lion.

DEMONIC SANCTIONS AND EMBARGOS MUST BREAK

Every siege over my life is broken into unrepairable pieces. Demonic sanctions and embargos come to a permanent end in Jesus' name.

354.   Job 38:11

When I said, "This far you may come, but no farther, And here your proud waves must stop!"

355.   Isaiah 14:4

That you will take up this proverb against the king of Babylon, and say: How the oppressor has ceased, the golden city ceased!

356.   Psalm 74:14

You broke the heads of Leviathan in pieces, And gave him as food to the people inhabiting the wilderness.

357.   Psalm 92:10

But my horn You have exalted like a wild ox; I have been anointed with fresh oil.

358.   Psalm 41:8

"An evil disease," they say, "cling to him. And now that he lies down, he will rise up no more."

359.   Proverbs 25:25

As cold water to a weary soul, so is good news from a far country.

360.   Job 42:10

And the Lord restored Job's losses when he prayed for his friends. Indeed the Lord gave Job twice as much as he had before.

361.   Psalm 30:11
You have turned for me my mourning into dancing; you have put off my sackcloth and clothed me with gladness.

362.   Zechariah 9:12
Return to the stronghold, you prisoners of hope. Even today I declare that I will restore double to you.

363.   Psalm 65:11
You crown the year with Your goodness, And your paths drip with abundance.

364.   Jeremiah 33:12
Thus says the Lord of hosts: 'In this place which is desolate without man and without beast, and in all its cities, there shall again be a dwelling place of shepherds causing their flocks to lie down.

365.   Revelation 5:5
But one of the elders said to me, "Do not weep. Behold, the Lion of the tribe of Judah, the Root of David, has prevailed to open the scroll and to loose its seven seals."

366.   Psalm 107:14
He brought them out of darkness and the shadow of death, And broke their chains in pieces.

367.   Isaiah 65:22

They shall not build and another inhabit; they shall not plant and another eat; for as the days of a tree, so shall be the days of My people, and My elect shall long enjoy the works of their hands.

368.   Isaiah 62:8-9

8 The Lord has sworn by His right hand and by the arm of His strength: "Surely I will no longer give your grain as food for your enemies; and the sons of the foreigner shall not drink your new wine, for which you have laboured.
9 But those who have gathered it shall eat it, and praise the Lord; those who have bought it together shall drink it in My holy courts.

369.   Job 2:3

Then the Lord said to Satan, "Have you considered My servant Job, that there is none like him on the earth, a blameless and upright man, one who fears God and shuns evil? And still he holds fast to his integrity, although you incited Me against him, to destroy him without cause."

370.   Hosea 14:2

Take words with you, and return to the Lord. Say to Him, "Take away all iniquity; receive us graciously, for we will offer the sacrifices of our lips."

YOUR NEW GARMENT FOR YOUR NEW SEASON

Lord, let this be the year/ the season that will change my story forever.

371. Matthew 9:16

No one puts a piece of unshrunk cloth on an old garment; for the patch pulls away from the garment, and the tear is made worse.

372. Matthew 22:12

So he said to him, 'Friend, how did you come in here without a wedding garment?' And he was speechless.

373. Isaiah 61:3

To console those who mourn in Zion,
To give them beauty for ashes,
The oil of joy for mourning,
The garment of praise for the spirit of heaviness;
That they may be called trees of righteousness,
The planting of the Lord, that He may be glorified."

374. Jeremiah 29:14

I will be found by you, says the Lord, and I will bring you back from your captivity; I will gather you from all the nations and from all the places where I have driven you, says the Lord, and I will bring you to the place from which I cause you to be carried away captive.

375. Isaiah 52:1

Awake, awake! Put on your strength, O Zion;

Put on your beautiful garments, O Jerusalem, the holy city!
For the uncircumcised and the unclean shall no longer come to
you.

376.   Ecclesiastes 9:8

Let your garments always be white, And let your head lack no oil.

377.   1 Peter 5:5

Likewise you younger people, submit yourselves to your elders.
Yes, all of you be submissive to one another, and be clothed with
humility, for "God resists the proud, But gives grace to the
humble."

378.   Mark 5:30

And Jesus, perceiving in himself that power had gone out from
him, immediately turned about in the crowd and said, "Who
touched my garments?"

379.   2 Kings 2:8

Then Elijah folded his cloak together and struck the water with it.
The river divided, and the two of them went across on dry ground!

380.   Exodus 31:10

and also the woven garments, both the sacred garments for Aaron
the priest and the garments for his sons when they serve as
priests,

381.   Zechariah 3:3-5

3 Now Joshua was dressed in filthy clothes as he stood before the
angel.

4 The angel said to those who were standing before him, "Take off his filthy clothes." Then he said to Joshua, "See, I have taken away your sin, and I will put fine garments on you."
5 Then I said, "Put a clean turban on his head." So they put a clean turban on his head and clothed him, while the angel of the Lord stood by.

382.   Jeremiah 52:33
So Jehoiachin changed from his prison garments, and he ate bread regularly before the king all the days of his life.

383.   Genesis 41:14
Then Pharaoh sent and called Joseph, and they brought him quickly out of the dungeon; and he shaved, changed his clothing, and came to Pharaoh.

384.   Genesis 41:42
Then Pharaoh took his signet ring off his hand and put it on Joseph's hand; and he clothed him in garments of fine linen and put a gold chain around his neck.

385.   Psalm 22:18
They divide My garments among them,
And for My clothing they cast lots.

No more Errors Prayers-
Cancelling Errors

Errors that keep taking me back to the beginning are cancelled forever in my life in Jesus' name

386.   Ecclesiastes 10:5
There is an evil I have seen under the sun,
As an error proceeding from the ruler:

387.   Matthew 6:10
Your kingdom come.
Your will be done
On earth as it is in heaven.

388.   Psalm 95:10
For forty years I was grieved with that generation, And said, 'It is a people who go astray in their hearts, And they do not know My ways.

389.   Jeremiah 23:32
Indeed, I am against those who prophesy false dreams,' declares the LORD. 'They tell them and lead my people astray with their reckless lies, yet I did not send or appoint them. They do not benefit these people in the least,' declares the LORD.

390.   2 Kings 6:5
But as one was felling a beam, the axe head fell into the water: and he cried, and said, Alas, master! for it was borrowed.

391.   Genesis 48:17

Now when Joseph saw that his father laid his right hand on the head of Ephraim, it displeased him; so he took hold of his father's hand to remove it from Ephraim's head to Manasseh's head.

392.   1 Chronicles 4:9

Now Jabez was more honourable than his brothers, and his mother called his name Jabez, saying, "Because I bore him in pain."

393.   Genesis 49:3-5

3 "Reuben, you are my firstborn,
My might and the beginning of my strength,
The excellency of dignity and the excellency of power.
4 Unstable as water, you shall not excel,
Because you went up to your father's bed;
Then you defiled it—
He went up to my couch.
5 "Simeon and Levi are brothers;
Instruments of cruelty are in their dwelling place.

394.   Deuteronomy 33:6 and verse 8

6 "Let Reuben live, and not die,
Nor let his men be few.
8 And of Levi he said:
"Let Your Thummim and Your Urim be with Your holy one,
Whom You tested at Massah,
And with whom You contended at the waters of Meribah,

395.   Esther 8:5

And said, "If it pleases the king, and if I have found favor in his sight and the thing seems right to the king and I am pleasing in his eyes, let it be written to revoke the letters devised by Haman, the son of Hammedatha the Agagite, which he wrote to annihilate the Jews who are in all the king's provinces.

396.   Psalm 116:8
For You have delivered my soul from death,
My eyes from tears,
And my feet from falling.

397.   Psalm 7:9
Oh, let the wickedness of the wicked come to an end,
But establish the just; For the righteous God tests the hearts and minds.

398.   Colossians 2:14
having wiped out the handwriting of requirements that was against us, which was contrary to us. And He has taken it out of the way, having nailed it to the cross.

399.   Job 23:10
But He knows the way that I take; When He has tested me, I shall come forth as gold.

400.   Psalm 37:23
The steps of a good man are ordered by the Lord, And He delights in his way.

401.   Psalm 40:2
He also brought me up out of a horrible pit, Out of the miry clay, And set my feet upon a rock, And established my steps.

402.   Genesis 27:33

Then Isaac trembled very violently and said, "Who was it then that hunted game and brought it to me, and I ate it all before you came, and I have blessed him? Yes, and he shall be blessed."

403.   Numbers 27:7-8

7 "The daughters of Zelophehad speak what is right; you shall surely give them a possession of inheritance among their father's brothers, and cause the inheritance of their father to pass to them. 8 And you shall speak to the children of Israel, saying: 'If a man dies and has no son, then you shall cause his inheritance to pass to his daughter.

Renunciation Prayers

Lord I renounce everything that stops your hand from intervening in my life.

404.   Romans 3:23

for all have sinned and fall short of the glory of God,

405.   Psalm 130:3

If you, LORD, kept a record of sins, Lord, who could stand?

406.   Psalm 143:2

Enter not into judgment with your servant, for no one living is righteous before you.

407.   Matthew 5:28

But I tell you that anyone who looks at a woman lustfully has already committed adultery with her in his heart.

408.   Job 31:1

"I have made a covenant with my eyes; Why then should I look upon a young woman?

409.   Romans 1:28-32

28 And even as they did not like to retain God in their knowledge, God gave them over to a debased mind, to do those things which are not fitting;

29 being filled with all unrighteousness, sexual immorality, wickedness, covetousness, maliciousness; full of envy, murder, strife, deceit, evil-mindedness; they are whisperers,

30 backbiters, haters of God, violent, proud, boasters, inventors of evil things, disobedient to parents,

31 undiscerning, untrustworthy, unloving, unforgiving, unmerciful;

32 who, knowing the righteous judgment of God, that those who practice such things are deserving of death, not only do the same but also approve of those who practice them.

410.   1 Corinthians 6:9-11

9 Do you not know that the unrighteous will not inherit the kingdom of God? Do not be deceived. Neither fornicators, nor idolaters, nor adulterers, nor homosexuals, nor sodomites,

10 nor thieves, nor covetous, nor drunkards, nor revilers, nor extortioners will inherit the kingdom of God.

11 And such were some of you. But you were washed, but you were sanctified, but you were justified in the name of the Lord Jesus and by the Spirit of our God.

411.   1 John 1:9

If we should confess our sins, He is faithful and just, that He may forgive us our sins and might cleanse us from all unrighteousness.

412.   Psalm51:2

Wash me clean of my iniquity and cleanse me from my sin.

1. **REJECTION**.
   I Renounce all rejection in my life. I decree and declare that I am accepted in the Lord/ I renounce the Spirit of fear/ I renounce every strongman of rejection / I renounce generational rejection / I renounce inherited rejection/ I renounce feeling unloved or I renounce thoughts of being aborted/ I renounce the feeling of not being accepted / I renounce self-hatred/I renounce low esteem/I renounce feeling inferior / I renounce all insecurity in Jesus name.

2. **PERVERSION:**
   I renounce all Sexual sin I have been involved in/ I renounce all molestation/ I renounce rape/ I renounce incest / I renounce Lust/ I renounce masturbation/ I renounce Adultery/ I renounce all fornication/ I renounce Lesbianism/ I renounce homosexuality/ I renounce lust of the eyes and lust of the flesh/ I renounce Prostitution/ I renounce the feeling of Guilt – shame- and condemnation- In Jesus Name.

3. **Sickness**
   I renounce all Diseases in body my mind or my soul. I renounce sickness/infirmity/Pain/Infection/ Hereditary/ Mind/Body/Back/ Skin/ Long term/short term- Anniversary sickness- Deaf/dam/Blind/ incurable diseases right now in Jesus name.

4. **Pride**
   I renounce all pride. I renounce the Leviathan spirit- I renounce Arrogance/ I renounce Ego/ I renounce Selfishness/ I renounce

Self-promotion/ I renounce Rebellion/ I renounce all
Competition I habe with self and others / I renounce feeling
Better than/ or above others in Juses name.

5. **Sadness**

   I renounce Loneliness/ I renounce Depression/ I renounce Self-
   pity/ I renounce Self demotion/ I renounce feeling unworthy in
   Jesus name.

6. **Strife**

   I renounce all Division/ I renounce Arguing/ I renounce
   Quarrelling/ I renounce Fighting/ I renounce Divorce/ I renounce
   Separation in Jesus name.

7. **Poverty**

   I renounce Poverty and Luck/ I renounce Debt/ I renounce
   insufficiency/ I renounce negativity/ I renounce slavery/
   renounce bondage/ joblessness/ sorry/ blocked blessing/

8. **Addiction**

   I renounce addiction to Smoking/ alcohol/ drugs/ foods/ caffeine/
   nicotine/ Marijuana and all other addictive things in Jesus name.

9. **Failure**

   I renounce Automatic failure mechanism in my life / I renounce
   falling/ I renounce closed door/ I renounce setback/ I renounce
   rejection / I renounce frustration/ I renounce repeating the same
   level / I renounce non-progression/ I renounce self-defeat in
   Jesus' name.

PROSPERITY DECLARATIONS
& DECREES

Bless me exceedingly and abundantly in this season.

413. Hosea 7:1
"When I would have healed Israel, Then the iniquity of Ephraim was uncovered, And the wickedness of Samaria. For they have committed fraud; A thief comes in; A band of robbers takes spoil outside.

414.   Isaiah 44:26
Who confirms the word of His servant,
And performs the counsel of His messengers;
Who says to Jerusalem, 'You shall be inhabited,'
To the cities of Judah, 'You shall be built,'
And I will raise up her waste places;

415.   Psalm 118:25
Save now, I pray, O LORD; O LORD, I pray, send now prosperity.

416.   Psalm 128:2
When you eat the labor of your hands, You shall be happy, and it shall be well with you.

417.   Leviticus 26:9
'I will look on you with favor and make you fruitful and increase your numbers, and I will keep my covenant with you.

418.   Jeremiah 30:19

There will be joy and songs of thanksgiving, and I will multiply my people, not diminish them; I will honor them, not despise them.

419.   2 Chronicles 9:22

King Solomon was greater in riches and wisdom than all the other kings of the earth. So King Solomon became richer and wiser than any other king on earth.

420.   Daniel 7:22

until the Ancient of Days came, and a judgment was made in favor of the saints of the Most High, and the time came for the saints to possess the kingdom.

421.   2 Chronicles 26:15

In Jerusalem he made machines of war invented by skillful men to be put on the towers and on the [corner] battlements for the purpose of shooting arrows and large stones. And his fame spread far, for he was marvelously helped until he was strong.

422.   Psalm 115:14

May the Lord give you increase more and more, You and your children.

423.   Psalm 44:3

For they did not gain possession of the land by their own sword,
Nor did their own arm save them;
But it was Your right hand, Your arm, and the light of Your countenance,
Because You favored them.

424.   Isaiah 43:19
Behold, I will do a new thing,
Now it shall spring forth;
Shall you not know it?
I will even make a road in the wilderness
And rivers in the desert.

425.   Psalm 112:3
Wealth and riches will be in his house,
And his righteousness endures forever.

426.   Deuteronomy 33:19
They shall call the peoples to the mountain;
There they shall offer sacrifices of righteousness;
For they shall partake of the abundance of the seas
And of treasures hidden in the sand."

427.   Psalm 68:19
Blessed be the Lord,
Who daily loads us with benefits,
The God of our salvation! Selah

428.   1 Samuel 3:11
Then the Lord said to Samuel: "Behold, I will do something in Israel at which both ears of everyone who hears it will tingle.

429.   1 Samuel 1:5
But to Hannah he would give a double portion, for he loved Hannah, although the Lord had closed her womb.

430.   Psalm 40:3

He has put a new song in my mouth—
Praise to our God;
Many will see it and fear,
And will trust in the Lord.

431.   Psalm 84:11

For the Lord God is a sun and shield;
The Lord will give grace and glory;
No good thing will He withhold
From those who walk uprightly.

432.   Genesis 30:22

Then God remembered Rachel, and God listened to her and opened her womb.

433.   Genesis 45:13

So you shall tell my father of all my glory in Egypt, and of all that you have seen; and you shall hurry and bring my father down here."

434.   Genesis 27:28

Therefore may God give you
Of the dew of heaven,
Of the fatness of the earth,
And plenty of grain and wine.

435.   Deuteronomy 30:3

that the Lord your God will bring you back from captivity, and have compassion on you, and gather you again from all the nations where the Lord your God has scattered you.

436.   Malachi 4:2

But to you who fear My name
The Sun of Righteousness shall arise
With healing in His wings;
And you shall go out
And grow fat like stall-fed calves.

437.   Ezekiel 12:23

Tell them therefore, 'Thus says the Lord God: "I will lay this
proverb to rest, and they shall no more use it as a proverb in
Israel." ' But say to them, ' "The days are at hand, and the
fulfillment of every vision.

438.   Isaiah 13:2

"Lift up a banner on the high mountain,
Raise your voice to them;
Wave your hand, that they may enter the gates of the nobles.

439.   Isaiah 35:1

The wilderness and the wasteland shall be glad for them,
And the desert shall rejoice and blossom as the rose;

440.   Deuteronomy 28:12

The Lord will open to you His good treasure, the heavens, to give
the rain to your land in its season, and to bless all the work of
your hand. You shall lend to many nations, but you shall not
borrow.

SHOOT – PRAYERS FOR AN IMMEDIATE BREAKTHROUGH

shoot an arrow into the heart of principalities blocking my lifting in Jesus name.

441.   2 Kings 13:17

When I said, "This far you may come, but no farther, And here your proud waves must stop!"

442.   Jeremiah 1:12

Then the Lord said to me, "You have seen well, for I am ready to perform My word."

443.   Psalm 149:5-7

5 Let his faithful people rejoice in this honor and sing for joy on their beds.
6 May the praise of God be in their mouths and a double-edged sword in their hands,
7 to inflict vengeance on the nations and punishment on the peoples,

444.   Jeremiah 50:14

"Put yourselves in array against Babylon all around,
All you who bend the bow;
Shoot at her, spare no arrows,
For she has sinned against the Lord.

445.   Psalm 64:7

But God shall shoot at them with an arrow;
Suddenly they shall be wounded.

446.   Psalm 144:6
Flash forth lightning and scatter them;
Shoot out Your arrows and destroy them.

447.   Isaiah 37:3
And they said to him, "Thus says Hezekiah: 'This day is a day of
trouble and rebuke and blasphemy; for the children have come to
birth, but there is no strength to bring them forth.

448.   1 Samuel 20:36
Then he said to his lad, "Now run, find the arrows which I shoot."
As the lad ran, he shot an arrow beyond him.

449.   Psalm 45:5
Your arrows are sharp in the heart of the King's enemies;
The peoples fall under You.

450.   Ezekiel 5:16
When I shoot at you with my deadly and destructive arrows of
famine, I will shoot to destroy you. I will bring more and more
famine upon you and cut off your supply of food.

451.   Jeremiah 51:11
Make the arrows bright!
Gather the shields!
The Lord has raised up the spirit of the kings of the Medes.
For His plan is against Babylon to destroy it,
Because it is the vengeance of the Lord,
The vengeance for His temple.

452.   Psalm 18:14

He sent out His arrows and scattered the foe,
Lightnings in abundance, and He vanquished them.

453.   Psalm 120:4

He will punish you with a warrior's sharp arrows, with burning
coals of the broom bush.

454.   Psalm 11:2

For look! The wicked bend their bow,
They make ready their arrow on the string,
That they may shoot secretly at the upright in heart.

455.   Psalm 38:2

For Your arrows pierce me deeply,
And Your hand presses me down.

456.   Psalm 7:13

He also prepares for Himself instruments of death;
He makes His arrows into fiery shafts.

FIRE – PRAYERS FOR AN IMMEDIATE BREAKTHROUGH

L et the fire of God fall from above. Let my enemies scatter as my breakthrough manifests.

457.　　　Lamentations 5:7
Our fathers sinned and are no more,
But we bear their iniquities

458.　　　Galatians 3:29
And if you are Christ's, then you are Abraham's seed, and heirs according to the promise.

459.　　　Hebrews 12:29
For our God is a consuming fire.

460.　　　Obadiah 1:18
The house of Jacob shall be a fire,
And the house of Joseph a flame;
But the house of Esau shall be stubble;
They shall kindle them and devour them,
And no survivor shall remain of the house of Esau,"
For the Lord has spoken.

461.　　　Genesis 19:24
Then the Lord rained brimstone and fire on Sodom and Gomorrah, from the Lord out of the heavens.

462.　　　Exodus 9:24

hail fell and lightning flashed back and forth. It was the worst
storm in all the land of Egypt since it had become a nation.

463.   2 Kings 1:10

So Elijah answered and said to the captain of fifty, "If I am a man
of God, then let fire come down from heaven and consume you
and your fifty men." And fire came down from heaven and
consumed him and his fifty.

464.   2 Kings 19:18

and have cast their gods into the fire; for they were not gods, but
the work of men's hands—wood and stone. Therefore they
destroyed them.

465.   Job 15:34

For the company of hypocrites will be barren,
And fire will consume the tents of bribery.

466.   Job 18:5

"The light of the wicked indeed goes out,
And the flame of his fire does not shine.

467.   Psalm 46:9

He makes wars cease to the end of the earth;
He breaks the bow and cuts the spear in two;
He burns the chariot in the fire.

468.   Psalm 66:12

He makes wars cease to the end of the earth;
He breaks the bow and cuts the spear in two;
He burns the chariot in the fire.

469.   Psalm 68:2

As smoke is driven away,
So drive them away;
As wax melts before the fire,
So let the wicked perish at the presence of God.

470.   Psalm 104:4

He makes winds his messengers, flames of fire his servants.

471.   Psalm 106:18

A fire was kindled in their company;
The flame burned up the wicked.

472.   Psalm 140:10

Let burning coals fall upon them;
Let them be cast into the fire,
Into deep pits, that they rise not up again.

473.   Proverbs 6:27

Can a man take fire to his bosom,
And his clothes not be burned?

474.   Isaiah 47:14

Behold, they shall be as stubble,
The fire shall burn them;
They shall not deliver themselves
From the power of the flame;
It shall not be a coal to be warmed by,
Nor a fire to sit before!

475.   Proverbs 25:22

For so you will heap coals of fire on his head,
And the Lord will reward you.

EVERYTHING HAS AN END.

LET DARKNESS COME TO END

O Lord let the darkness in my life come to an end. You are my LIGHT

476.   Job 28:3
Man puts an end to darkness,
And searches every recess
For ore in the darkness and the shadow of death.

477.   Job 8:7
Though your beginning was small,
Yet your latter end would increase abundantly.

478.   Psalm 46:9
He makes wars cease to the end of the earth;
He breaks the bow and cuts the spear in two;
He burns the chariot in the fire.

479.   Jude 1:9
Yet Michael the archangel, in contending with the devil, when he disputed about the body of Moses, dared not bring against him a reviling accusation, but said, "The Lord rebuke you!"

480.   Psalm 7:9
Oh, let the wickedness of the wicked come to an end,
But establish the just;

For the righteous God tests the hearts and minds.

481.   Psalm 39:4
"Lord, make me to know my end,
And what is the measure of my days,
That I may know how frail I am.

482.   Psalm 90:10
Our days may come to seventy years,
* or eighty, if our strength endures;*
yet the best of them are but trouble and sorrow,
* for they quickly pass, and we fly away.*

483.   Psalm 73:17
Until I went into the sanctuary of God;
Then I understood their end.

484.   Psalm 106:32
They angered Him also at the waters of strife,
So that it went ill with Moses on account of them;

485.   Nahum 1:9
What do you conspire against the Lord?
He will make an utter end of it.
Affliction will not rise up a second time.

486.   Hosea 1:4
Then the Lord said to him:
"Call his name Jezreel,
For in a little while
I will avenge the bloodshed of Jezreel on the house of Jehu,
And bring an end to the kingdom of the house of Israel.

487.   Ecclesiastes 7:8

The end of a thing is better than its beginning;
The patient in spirit is better than the proud in spirit.

488.   Proverbs 14:12

There is a way that appears to be right, but in the end it leads to
death.

489.   Ezekiel 7:3

Now the end has come upon you,
And I will send My anger against you;
I will judge you according to your ways,
And I will repay you for all your abominations.

490.   Habakkuk 2:3

For the vision is yet for an appointed time;
But at the end it will speak, and it will not lie.
Though it tarries, wait for it;
Because it will surely come,
It will not tarry.

491.   Isaiah 10:1

"Woe to those who decree unrighteous decrees,
Who write misfortune,
Which they have prescribed

492.   Isaiah 14:4

that you will take up this proverb against the king of Babylon, and
say:
"How the oppressor has ceased,
The golden city ceased!

493.   Isaiah 41:11

"Behold, all those who were incensed against you
Shall be ashamed and disgraced;
They shall be as nothing,
And those who strive with you shall perish.

494.   1 Samuel 30:18-19

18 So David recovered all that the Amalekites had carried away,
and David rescued his two wives.
19 And nothing of theirs was lacking, either small or great, sons
or daughters, spoil or anything which they had taken from them;
David recovered all.

495.   Zechariah 9:11-12

11 "As for you also,
Because of the blood of your covenant,
I will set your prisoners free from the waterless pit.
12 Return to the stronghold,
You prisoners of hope.
Even today I declare
That I will restore double to you.

MYSTERY OF THE FOUR WINDS PRAYERS

On account of the blood of Jesus, let the winds work in my favour from this day going forward.

496. Psalm 104:4 **NORTH WIND OF GODS PRESENCE**
He makes winds his messengers, flames of fire his servants.

497. Psalm 18:10
He mounted the cherubim and flew; he soared on the wings of the wind.

498. Acts 2:2
*And suddenly there came a sound from heaven, as of a rushing mighty wind, and it **filled the whole house where they were sitting.***

499. 2 Kings 2:11
Then it happened, as they continued on and talked, that suddenly a chariot of fire appeared with horses of fire, and separated the two of them; and Elijah went up by a whirlwind into heaven.

500. Psalm 75:6
6 For exaltation comes neither from the east Nor from the west nor from the south.
7 But God is the Judge: He puts down one, And exalts another.

501. Exodus 10:12 **EAST WIND OF DESTRUCTION**
And the Lord said unto Moses, Stretch out thine hand over the land of Egypt for the locusts, that they may come up upon the land

of Egypt, and eat every herb of the land, even all that the hail hath left.

502.   Exodus 14:21

And Moses stretched out his hand over the sea; and the Lord caused the sea to go back by a strong east wind all that night, and made the sea dry land, and the waters were divided.

503.   Exodus 10:19 **WEST WIND OF DELIVERANCE**

And the Lord turned a mighty strong west wind, which took away the locusts, and cast them into the Red sea; there remained not one locust in all the coasts of Egypt.

504.   Exodus 14:26

And the Lord said unto Moses, Stretch out thine hand over the sea, that the waters may come again upon the Egyptians, upon their chariots, and upon their horsemen.

505.   Psalm 35:5

Let them be as chaff before the wind: and let the angel of the Lord chase them.

506.   Psalm 78:26-29   **SOUTH WIND OF DIVINE PROVISION**

26 He caused an east wind to blow in the heavens;
And by His power He brought in the south wind.
27 He also rained meat on them like the dust,
Feathered fowl like the sand of the seas;
28 And He let them fall in the midst of their camp,
All around their dwellings.
29 So they ate and were well filled,
For He gave them their own desire.

507.   Genesis 41:6
Then behold, seven thin heads, blighted by the east wind, sprang up after them.

508.   Genesis 8:1
Then God remembered Noah, and every living thing, and all the animals that were with him in the ark. And God made a wind to pass over the earth, and the waters subsided.

509.   Exodus 15:10
But you blew with your breath, and the sea covered them.
They sank like lead in the mighty waters.

510.   Numbers 11:31
Now a wind went out from the Lord, and it brought quail from the sea and left them fluttering near the camp, about a day's journey on this side and about a day's journey on the other side, all around the camp, and about two cubits above the surface of the ground.

511.   1 Kings 18:41
Then Elijah said to Ahab, "Go up, eat and drink; for there is the sound of abundance of rain."

512.   Job 27:21
The east wind carries him away, and he is gone;
It sweeps him out of his place.

513.   Job 30:22
You lift me up to the wind and cause me to ride on it;
You spoil my success.

514.   Job 37:17

Why are your garments hot,
When He quiets the earth by the south wind?

515.   Job 38:24

By what way is light diffused,
Or the east wind scattered over the earth?

516.   Psalm 1:4

Not so the wicked! They are like chaff that the wind blows away.

517.   Psalm 18:10

He mounted the cherubim and flew;
*   he soared on the wings of the wind.*

SPECIAL THANKS

Vanessa Moona for putting this in book format

Taonga Mutambo and Oluwabukunmi Kolawole for scripture edits and typing.

The Lord bless you a thousand times more

Lastly, I would like to thank, my daughter Crystal, for the cover works and layout.

Love you to infinity and beyond

Printed in Great Britain
by Amazon

40545712R00066